THE ESSENTIAL COLLECTION

HANDEL

GOLD

Published by:
Chester Music Limited,
8/9 Frith Street, London W1D 3JB, England.

Exclusive Distributors:
Music Sales Limited,
Distribution Centre, Newmarket Road, Bury St. Edmunds, Suffolk IP33 3YB, England.
Music Sales Corporation,
257 Park Avenue South, New York, NY10010, United States of America.
Music Sales Pty Limited,
120 Rothschild Avenue, Rosebery, NSW 2018, Australia.

Order No. CH66792
ISBN 1-84449-062-9
This book © Copyright 2003 by Chester Music.

Printed in the United Kingdom.

Your Guarantee of Quality:
As publishers, we strive to produce every book to the highest commercial standards.
The music has been carefully designed to minimise awkward page turns
and to make playing from it a real pleasure.
Particular care has been given to specifying acid-free, neutral-sized
paper made from pulps which have not been elemental chlorine bleached.
This pulp is from farmed sustainable forests and was produced
with special regard for the environment.
Throughout, the printing and binding have been planned to ensure a sturdy,
attractive publication which should give years of enjoyment.
If your copy fails to meet our high standards, please inform us and we will gladly replace it.

www.musicsales.com

CHESTER MUSIC
part of the Music Sales Group

London/New York/Paris/Sydney/Copenhagen/Berlin/Madrid/Tokyo

I Will Magnify Thee
(from Belshazzar)

Composed by George Frideric Handel

Allegretto

See, The Conqu'ring Hero Comes
(from Judas Maccabaeus)

Composed by George Frideric Handel

Alla marcia

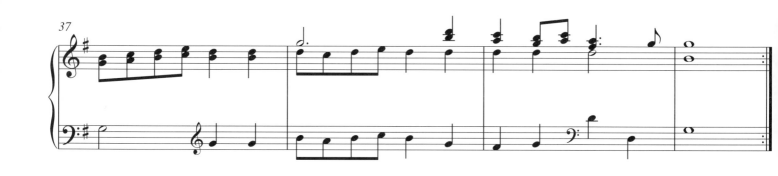

poco rall.

Zadok The Priest
(Coronation Anthem)

Composed by George Frideric Handel

Andante maestoso

mp sempre cresc.

Ev'ry Valley Shall Be Exalted
(from Messiah)

Composed by George Frideric Handel

Hallelujah Chorus
(from Messiah)

Composed by George Frideric Handel

23

24

I Know That My Redeemer Liveth
(from Messiah)

Composed by George Frideric Handel

Larghetto

poco rit.   a tempo

Let The Bright Seraphim
(from Samson)

Composed by George Frideric Handel

35

Dead March
(from Saul)

Composed by George Frideric Handel

The Arrival of the Queen of Sheba
(from Solomon)

Composed by George Frideric Handel

Allegro

Lascia Ch'io Pianga
(from Rinaldo)

Composed by George Frideric Handel

Largo

a tempo

Art Thou Troubled?

(from Rodelinda)

Composed by George Frideric Handel

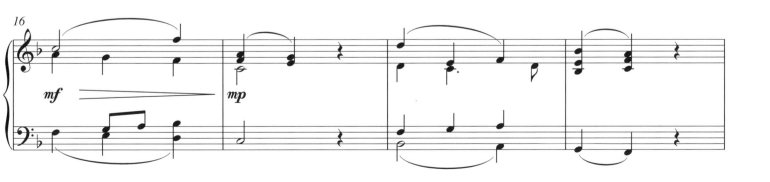

rall.

D.S. al Coda

𝄋 CODA

47

Largo
(from Serse)

Composed by George Frideric Handel

Aylesford Piece

Composed by George Frideric Handel

Invention in G major

Composed by George Frideric Handel

Boureé in G major

Composed by George Frideric Handel

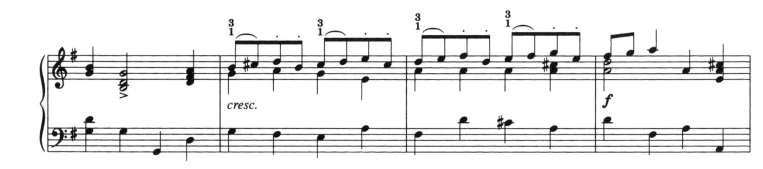

53

Chaconne in G major
(Theme and Six Variations)
Composed by George Frideric Handel

Fantasia in A major

Composed by George Frideric Handel

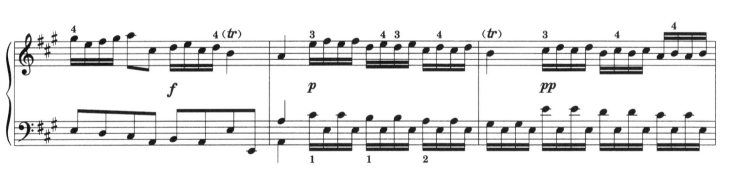

Gavotte in B♭ major

Composed by George Frideric Handel

Allegro con spirito

Intermezzo
L'istesso tempo

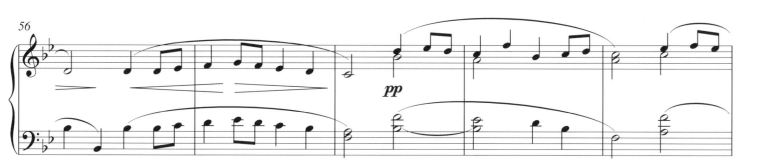

Gavotte

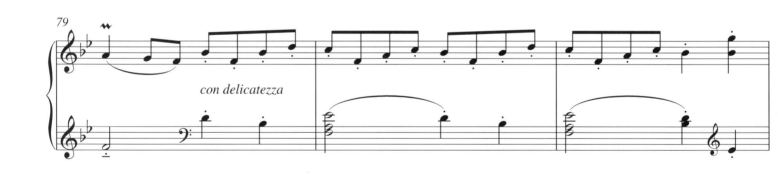

Sarabande
(from Harpsichord Suite in D minor)

Composed by George Frideric Handel

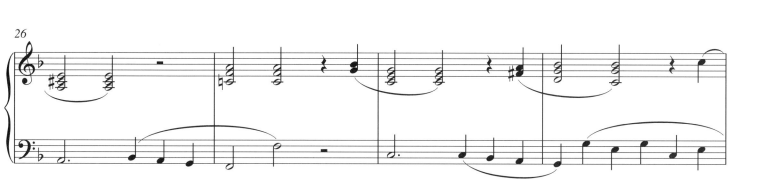

molto rit.

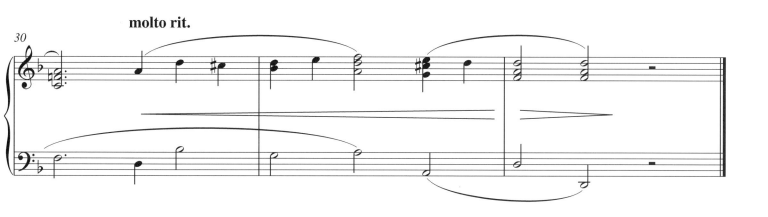

Suite No.7
(Allegro)

Composed by George Frideric Handel

Organ Concerto in F major
'The Cuckoo and the Nightingale'
(Allegro)

Composed by George Frideric Handel

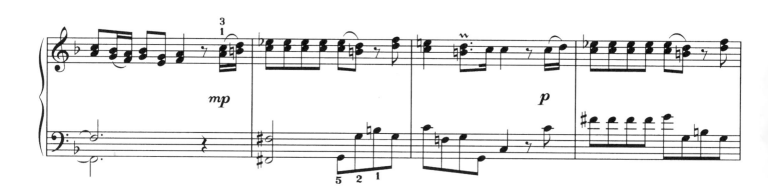

Harp Concerto in B♭ major
(Allegro moderato)
Composed by George Frideric Handel

Allegro moderato (♩=88)

The Harmonious Blacksmith
(Air and Variations)

Composed by George Frideric Handel

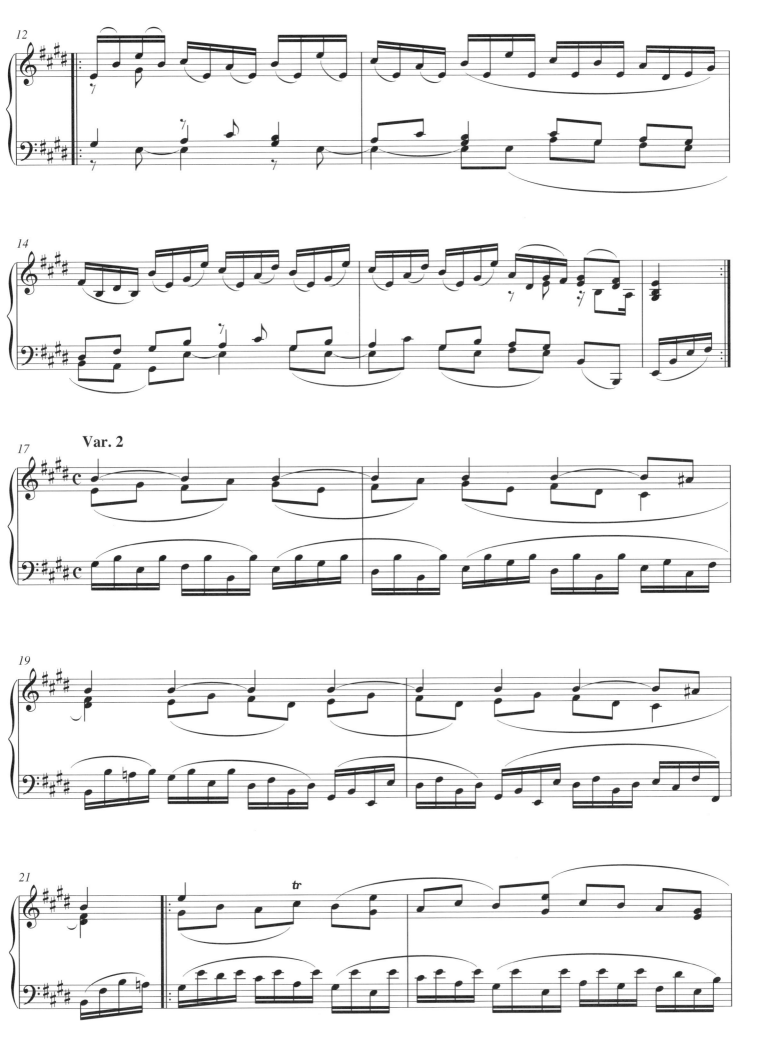

Var. 3

legato

Air
(from Water Music)

Composed by George Frideric Handel

Allegro
(from Water Music)

Composed by George Frideric Handel

Allegro (♩ = 132)

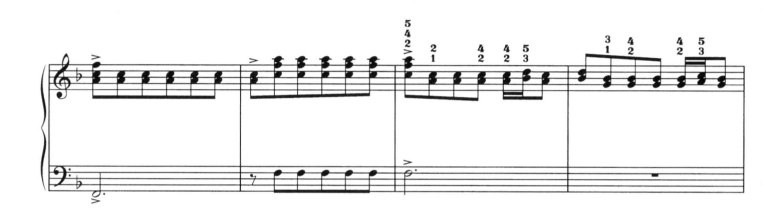

Hornpipe
(from Water Music)

Composed by George Frideric Handel

Alla hornpipe

Siciliana
(from Music for the Royal Fireworks)

Composed by George Frideric Handel

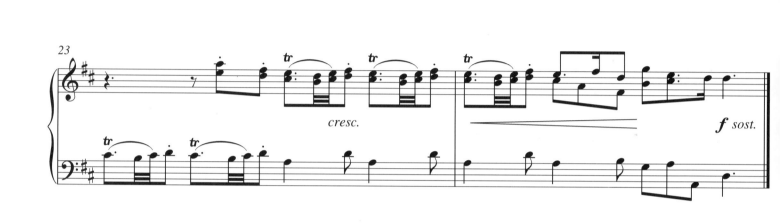